I Can Draw POLAR Animals

Please visit our web site at: www.garethstevens.com
For a free color catalog describing Gareth Stevens' list of high-quality books and multimedia programs, call 1-800-542-2595 (USA) or 1-800-461-9120 (Canada). Gareth Stevens Publishing's Fax: (414) 332-3567.

Library of Congress Cataloging-in-Publication Data

Leroux-Hugon, Hélène.
    [Animaux du froid. English]
    I can draw polar animals / by Hélène Leroux-Hugon.
       p. cm. — (I can draw animals!)
    Includes bibliographical references and index.
    ISBN 0-8368-2840-2 (lib. bdg.)
    1. Polar animals in art—Juvenile literature. 2. Drawing—Technique—Juvenile
literature. [1. Polar animals in art. 2. Drawing—Technique.] I. Title.
    NC783.8.P65L4713   2001
    743.6—dc21   00-053146

This edition first published in 2001 by
Gareth Stevens Publishing
A World Almanac Education Group Company
330 West Olive Street, Suite 100
Milwaukee, Wisconsin 53212 USA

This U.S. edition © 2001 by Gareth Stevens, Inc. Original edition first published by Larousse-Bordas, Paris, France, under the title *Les animaux du Froid*, © Dessain et Tolra/HER 2000. Additional end matter © 2001 by Gareth Stevens, Inc.

Illustrations: Hélène Leroux-Hugon
Photography: Cactus Studio
Translation: Valerie J. Weber
English text: Valerie J. Weber
Gareth Stevens editor: Katherine Meitner
Cover design: Katherine Kroll

Printed in the United States of America

  2 3 4 5 6 7 8 9 05 04 03 02

I Can Draw
POLAR
Animals

Hélène Leroux-Hugon

Gareth Stevens Publishing
A WORLD ALMANAC EDUCATION GROUP COMPANY

Table of Contents

I Can Draw

Observing

Before you start drawing these animals from the polar regions, gather some photos and books about them. If possible, go to a zoo to visit them. Look at each animal carefully, without pencil or paper, to see how they are formed. Try to find simple geometric shapes, such as ovals or circles, in these animals.

Practicing

Without a stencil or a compass, draw circles, ovals, and curves by hand. This is called freestyle drawing. Notice that a circle can be more or less regular, that an oval can be wide or narrow, long or short.

Drawing by Steps

Choose your model in this book, for example, the seal.

1 The seal is made from a big oval for the body and a smaller one for the head (see page 10). Step by step, draw the form with a light mark. At first, of course, your drawing will be simple. This stage is called a sketch; it helps you decide upon the size of the head compared to the size of the body, and where you can accurately place each body part.

2 Add the details, such as the rear flippers, which look like a tail. Don't press too hard on your pencil; you're going to make several marks on the paper before deciding which one you like the best. You will have to erase the marks that are indicated by the dotted lines on the model.

3 Finish your design by tracing the eye, nostril, whiskers, and front paw. Look at the model and redraw the outline, making the lines smoother and more lively. That way, you can make your seal drawing look more like a real seal.

Now you're free to color in the drawing. You'll also be able to add other animals to your drawing, including details about their habitats.

While you are drawing, you will also learn many things about animals and their natural habitats. Look at the footprint from each animal at the bottom of the page — for example, the polar bear.

Some animals may not have a footprint. This is true for the walrus, which travels with its fins on a sheet of ice, and, of course, for the whale. In that case, you will find a tiny drawing of the animal at the bottom of the page. Here, for example, is the seal.

Polar Bears in Winter

1 Draw a large oval for the body and a pear shape for the head.

2 You are now going to draw the legs. The dots show the lines you should erase.

3 Look at the example and add the muzzle, the eye, the ear, the tail, and the wavy fur.

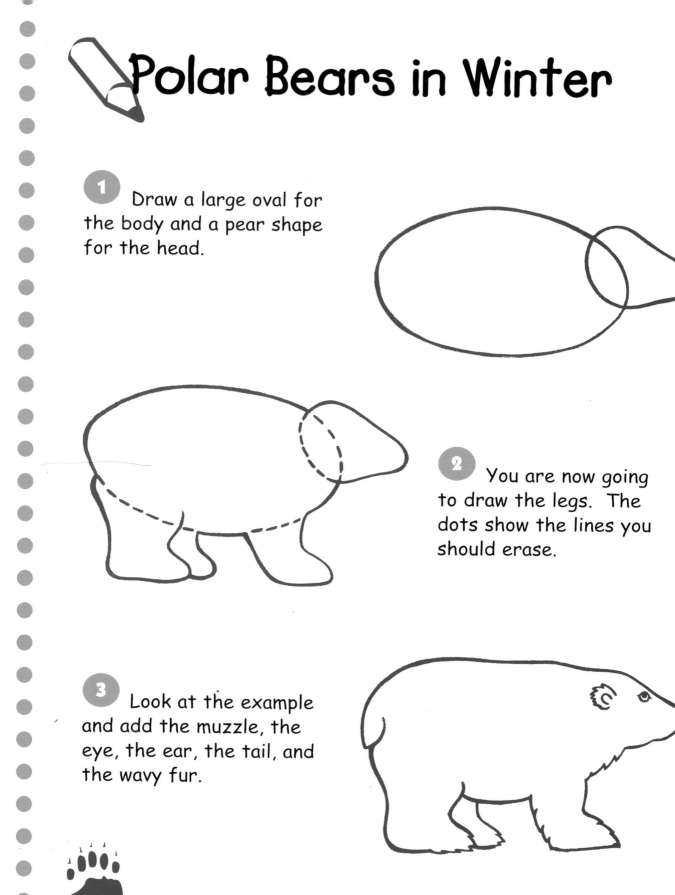

The polar bear is well adapted to its life on the ice floes. It has webbed feet for swimming and can walk long distances.

To protect itself from the cold, polar bears hibernate in shelters deep in the snow. They eat seals and fish.

Seal Family

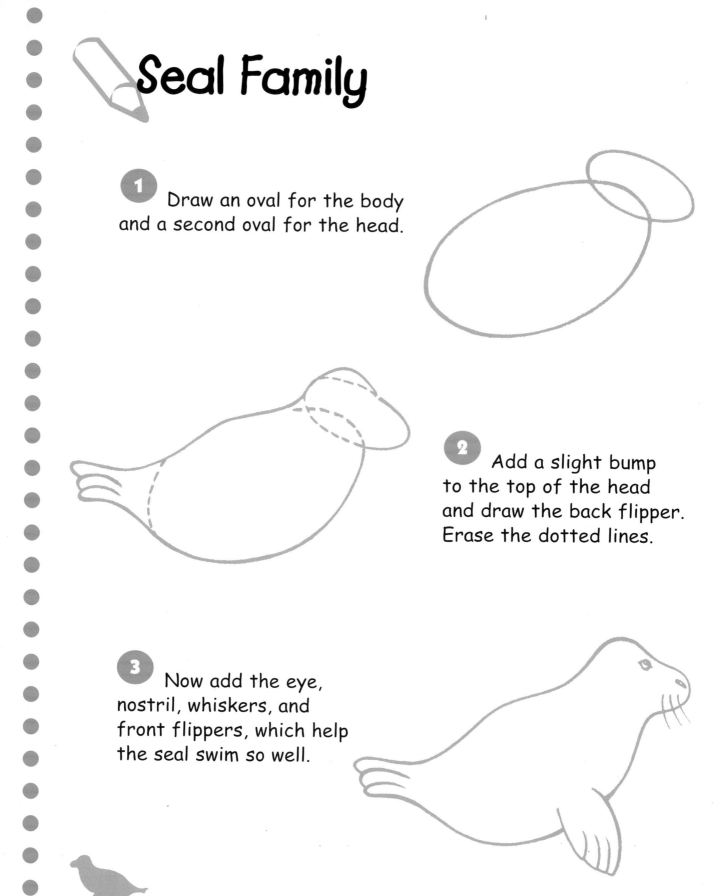

1. Draw an oval for the body and a second oval for the head.

2. Add a slight bump to the top of the head and draw the back flipper. Erase the dotted lines.

3. Now add the eye, nostril, whiskers, and front flippers, which help the seal swim so well.

The seal lives along the coast and in the open sea. It slides into the water and swims under the ice. The seal makes a hole in the ice so it can come up to the surface to breathe. Some species of seals live at the South Pole in Antarctica.

Walruses on Ice

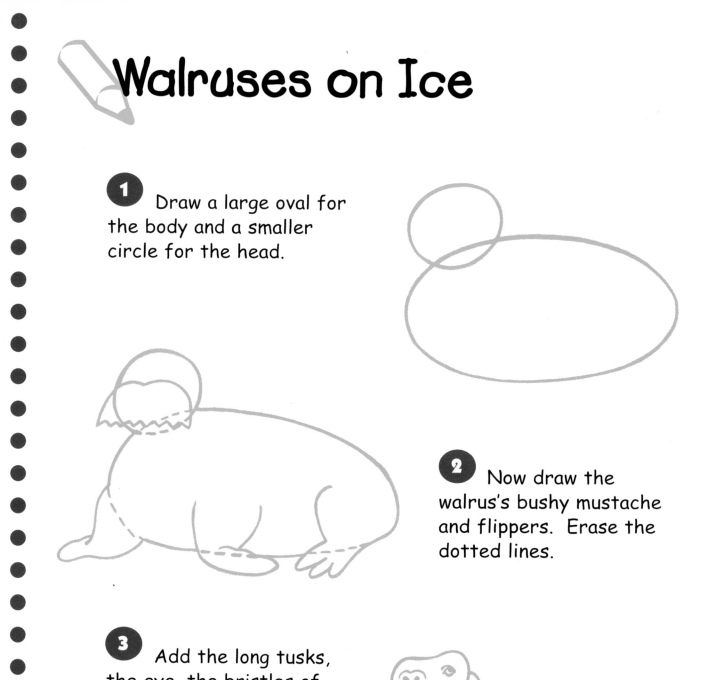

1 Draw a large oval for the body and a smaller circle for the head.

2 Now draw the walrus's bushy mustache and flippers. Erase the dotted lines.

3 Add the long tusks, the eye, the bristles of the mustache, and the nostrils. Don't forget the rolls of fat on this big guy!

The walrus has two enormous canine teeth, called tusks, that can reach up to 3 feet (1 meter) in length. The tusks allow the walrus to pull itself up onto the ice or defend itself from predators. Walruses eat fish, crustaceans, and clams.

13

The Arctic

The Arctic is an ocean covered with an immense sheet of floating ice at the North Pole. Sometimes, huge blocks of ice fall from this sheet. The biggest blocks are called icebergs. The Artic is a difficult place in which to live — the winters are long, and the temperatures are low. The animals who live here are well adapted to the cold, protected by fur and a thick layer of fat.

Musk Ox

1 Draw a large oval for the body and a little one for the head.

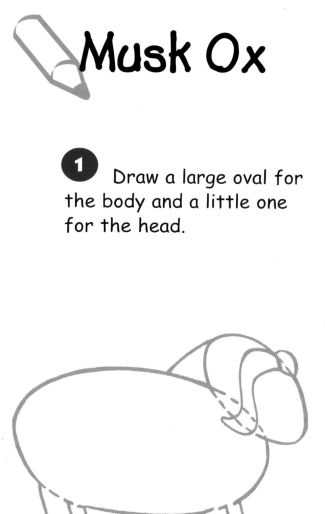

2 Notice where the horns, the neck, and the legs are. The dots indicate the lines you may erase.

3 Look at this model and add the eye and the muzzle. Finish the legs and hooves. Sketch warm fur on the outline of the body.

16

Musk oxen live in small herds. Their fur allows them to endure very cold temperatures, sometimes below –40°F (-40°C).

In winter, when snow covers the ground, the musk ox eats lichens; in summer, it eats tree sprouts, leaves, and grasses.

17

The Big Bad Wolf

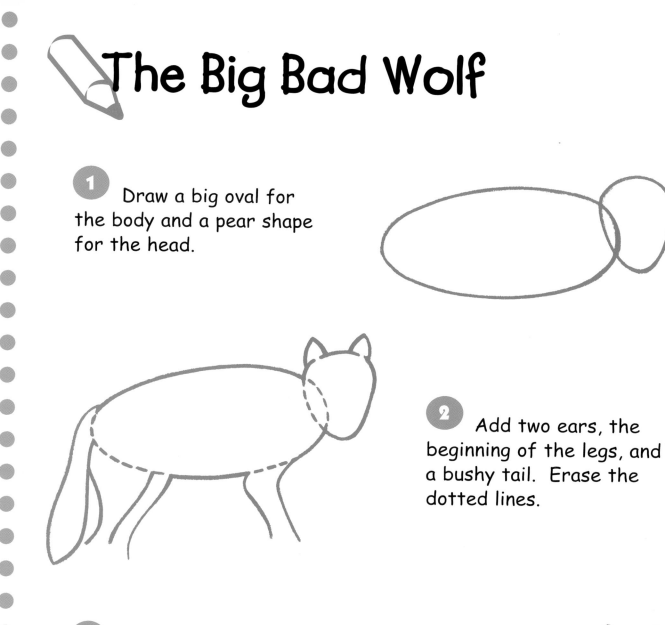

1 Draw a big oval for the body and a pear shape for the head.

2 Add two ears, the beginning of the legs, and a bushy tail. Erase the dotted lines.

3 Now draw the eyes and the muzzle and finish the legs and paws. Redraw the outline as well as you can. What a beautiful, wild animal you've drawn!

One way you can recognize the wolf is by its bushy tail and slanting eyes. In winter, it lives in bands of up to ten wolves.

Wolves are great predators and often run long distances to hunt all kinds of animals. They usually prey on weak or old animals.

Reindeer of the Tundra

1 Sketch a long oval for the body, a small oval for the head, and two lines for the neck.

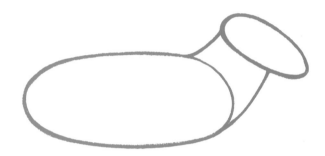

2 Start drawing the reindeer's legs and antlers and add the ear. Erase the dotted lines.

3 Finish drawing the majestic antlers, legs, and hooves. Don't forget the eye, the little tail, and the muzzle with its nostril.

20

The reindeer lives in groups, called herds, on the tundra. In winter, it finds its food by scratching through the snow with its big hooves. In summer, it eats grasses and lichens. Both male and female reindeer have horns that fall off once a year.

The Tundra

The tundra is a huge plain in the northernmost regions of North American, Europe, and Asia. Because of its extreme cold, the tundra ground is deeply frozen throughout one part of the year. Only moss and lichen grow here. Forests of conifer trees grow in the southern area.

When wolves attack, the musk oxen move into a circle. They face outward to defend themselves from the wolves' sharp teeth.

23

Party Penguins

1 Sketch a large oval for the body, then add a little oval for the head.

2 Draw a pointy beak, a tiny tail, and the foot. Erase the dotted lines at both the top and the bottom.

3 Add details to the beak and the foot. Draw the eye, the wing, and the sharp line of the feathers. Don't you think your penguin looks dressed for a party?

24

Emperor penguins live in groups in the open sea and only come to land to reproduce. The female penguin lays one egg in winter.

Once the egg hatches, the parents keep their little one warm between their feet and their tummy.

25

The Sea Elephant

1 Draw two ovals — a big one for the body and a little one for the head — and two lines for the neck.

2 Draw two bumps on the head, then the nose and the mouth. Sketch the flippers. Use your eraser to rub out the dotted lines.

3 Look at this example to improve your design, then add the eye, the nostrils, and the teeth. Don't forget the rolls of fat!

26

The sea elephant has a long, floppy nose in the shape of an elephant's trunk. This big nose lets the sea elephant's cries be heard from far away. The male is huge; it can grow up to 20 feet (6 m) long and weigh more than 3 tons! It eats squid and fish.

Traveling Albatross

1 Draw a large oval for the body, then add a little circle for the head and two lines for the neck.

2 Sketch the wing and the tail. Then add the feet. The dots show which lines you should erase.

3 Add the eye and the beak. Finish the drawing by adding in the feathers of this great traveler.

28

The albatross is a huge bird with a wingspan of almost 12 feet (3.5 m). It can live at sea for months at a time by sleeping on ice floes and feeding on marine animals. The albatross only comes to the coastline to build a nest and raise its babies.

A Frozen Land

As opposed to the Arctic, Antarctica is a continent located at the South Pole, surrounded by frozen seas. The main part of Antarctica is covered with snow that doesn't melt, even in summer. This is the coldest and windiest place on Earth. Almost no land animals live there. Most animals live in the sea, where they can find lots of food.

The Whale and Its Calf

1 Draw a large oval for the body.

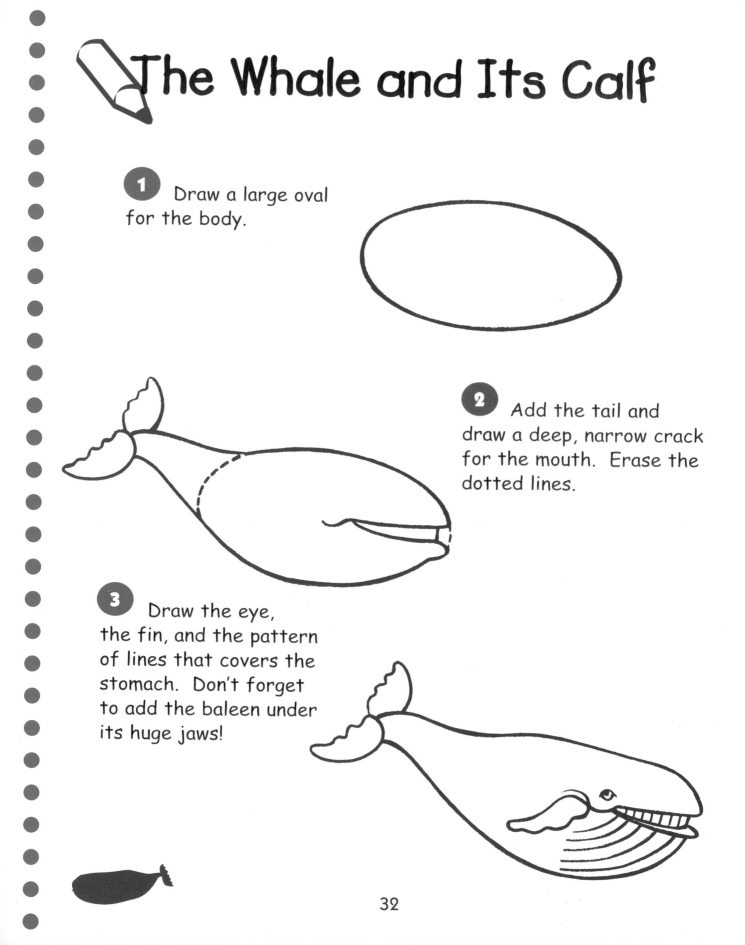

2 Add the tail and draw a deep, narrow crack for the mouth. Erase the dotted lines.

3 Draw the eye, the fin, and the pattern of lines that covers the stomach. Don't forget to add the baleen under its huge jaws!

The blue whale lives in all the cold seas on Earth. It's the largest of living animals. It can grow to nearly 100 feet (30 m) long and weigh up to 150 tons (135 metric tons). To breathe, the blue whale must return to the surface of the water.

Funny Narwhal

1 For the body, draw a long, egg-shaped form.

2 Now add the fin, tail, and mouth. Then try to make the whole outline smoother. Erase the dotted line.

3 Draw the eye and then the long tusk, making spirals around it. Look, the narwhal is smiling at you!

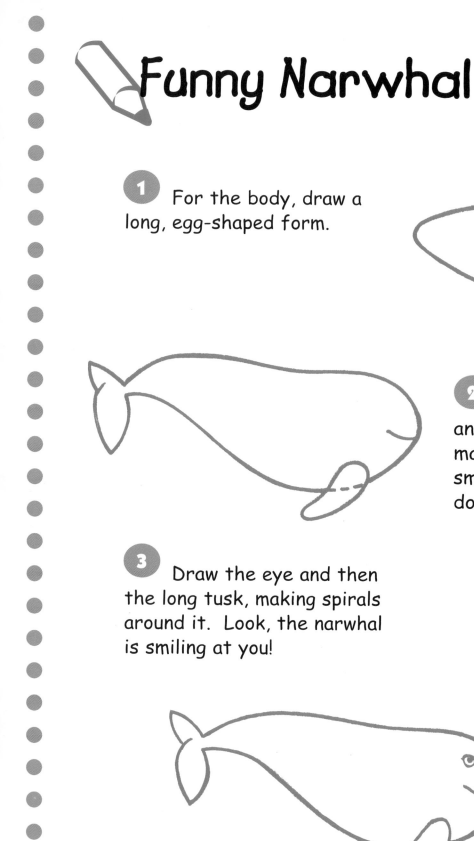

The male narwhal's tooth, or tusk, grows on its upper lip and can reach 10 feet (3 m) long. The narwhal uses its tusk to defend itself from predators such as sharks and other whales. It lives in the cold Arctic seas, eating fish and squid.

Oceans

Even though the water temperature never goes down below 28°F (-2°C), the ocean life near the North and South Poles is the richest life on Earth. In these cold, polar waters, tiny shrimp, called krill, and plankton provide food for many animals, including the huge blue whale.

More to Read and View

Books about Drawing

I Can Draw That!: Easy Animals and Monsters (Books and Stuff). Robert Pierce (Grosset & Dunlap)

I Can Draw That, Too!: People, Places, and Things (Books and Stuff). Robert Pierce (Grosset & Dunlap)

Kids Can Draw Animals (Kids Can Draw). Philippe Legendre (Walter Foster)

Learn to Draw for Ages Six and Up. Nina Kidd (Lowell House)

Mark Kistler's Draw Squad. Mark Kistler (Fireside)

Mark Kistler's Imagination Station/Learn How to Draw in 3-D with Public Television's Favorite Drawing Teacher. Mark Kistler (Fireside)

Videos

Doodle: Drawing Animals (A & F Video)

Dan Mahuta: Drawing Made Easy (A & F Video)

Web Sites

Learn to Draw: tqjunior.thinkquest.org

Learn to Draw with Billy Bear: www.billybear4kids.com

Some web sites stay current longer than others. To find additional web sites, enter key words based on animals and habitats you've read about in this book, such as *polar bear, seal, penguin, walrus, reindeer, musk ox, narwhal, Arctic,* and *Antarctica.*

Glossary/Index

You can find these words on the pages listed.

adapt — to change to suit one's specific conditions or surroundings 9, 15

Antarctica — the continent at the South Pole; it's almost completely covered with ice year-round 11, 31

Arctic — an ice-covered region surrounding the North Pole 15, 31, 35

baleen — the horny material forming fringed plates that hang from the upper jaw of baleen whales 32

bristle — a short, stiff hair 12

canine — a pointed tooth that is shaped somewhat like a cone 13

compass — a tool that helps draw circles. A compass has two arms — one that is placed at the center of the circle and another that holds a pencil 6

conifer — a tree or shrub that has needles instead of flat leaves. Many conifers have cones and are green year-round. Pines, spruces, and firs are all conifer trees 23

continent — one of seven large land areas on Earth. They are Asia, Africa, North America, South America, Antarctica, Europe, and Australia 31

crustacean — an animal that has a hard shell and lives mostly in the water 13

endure — to put up with something, to be able to stand it 17

habitats — the places where animals or plants live or grow 7

hibernate — to spend winter in a state like sleep 9

iceberg — a large piece of floating ice. Icebergs break off of glaciers 15

ice floe — a flat area of floating ice 9, 29

immense — huge; of enormous size 15

lichen — a plant without flowers that grows on tree trunks, rocks, or on the ground 17, 21, 23

marine — living in the sea 29

muzzle — part of an animal's head that includes its nose, mouth, and jaws 8, 16, 18, 20

plankton — tiny plants and animals that float in the sea or another body of water. Many sea animals, both huge and tiny, eat plankton 37

polar — having to do with the North or South Poles 6, 8

predator — an animal that hunts other animals for food 13, 19, 35

prey — to hunt for food 19

reproduce — to produce offspring. Animals reproduce by having babies or laying eggs 25

species — a group of animals or plants that have certain features in common 11

stencil — a sheet of plastic or cardboard with a design cut into it used to draw specific shapes or patterns 6

tundra — a huge, treeless plain in the Arctic 21, 23

wingspan — the distance between the tip of one wing and the tip of the other wing when both are fully spread out 29